THE LITTLE BOOK OF
CANADA

Published in 2024 by OH!
An Imprint of Welbeck Non-Fiction Limited,
part of Welbeck Publishing Group.
Offices in: London – 20 Mortimer Street, London W1T 3JW
and Sydney – Level 17, 207 Kent St, Sydney NSW 2000 Australia
www.welbeckpublishing.com

Compilation text © Welbeck Non-Fiction Limited 2023
Design © Welbeck Non-Fiction Limited 2023

ISBN 978-1-80069-413-2

Compiled and written by: Dave Verey and Nick Hammond
Editorial: Saneaah Muhammad
Design: Tony Seddon
Project manager: Russell Porter
Production: Arlene Lestrade

A CIP catalogue record for this book is available from the British Library

Printed in Dubai

10 9 8 7 6 5 4 3 2 1

THE LITTLE BOOK OF
CANADA

A LAND OF
BREATHTAKING BEAUTY

CONTENTS

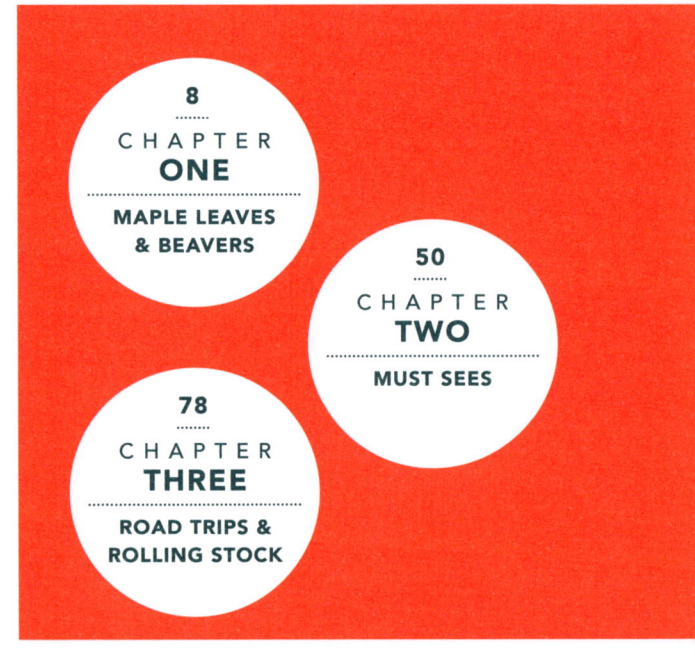

INTRODUCTION

When it comes to Canada, just the you've-never-seen-it-before scenery would be enough. Fjord-slashed coastlines, glacier-fed blue lakes, majestic prairies, ancient forests, treeless tundra, and towering ranges. Count it out: 46 national parks, 42 rivers, 21,000 mountains, and more lakes than the rest of the world combined.

It's an outdoor playground: you can hike, bike, canoe, fish, hunt, birdwatch, raft, climb, and even hold your own personal photoshoot in front of mind-blowing landscapes. And yes, you can fulfil your bucket-list skiing dreams with the world's longest season, great powder, and first-class resorts.

But whether you're landing a bush plane on a glacier or a 1440 on the half pipe, you'll need to eat, and Canada is the melting pot for international cuisine. Plus, there's nowhere better for fresh-cold water seafood, I'm talking wild salmon and velvety scallops… not to mention the lobster.

To get across the country, you have the choice of truly iconic road trips or once in a lifetime train journeys. Wherever you find yourself, be sure to keep an eye out for bears, moose, cougars, eagles, and any other furry friends hanging about.

Lest we forget that Canada is one of the most culturally diverse countries in the world, and its rich history can be experienced in abundance. The Indigenous tribes of the original land, renowned for their artistry and unique cultures, still form an intrinsic part of the modern nation.

Explore galleries, visit historical sites and islands, celebrate festivals, and walk ancient trails to see Canada from the perspective of those who know it best.

One thing's for sure in this fascinating country, you can expect a friendly welcome from a proud people that you can't help but like.

CHAPTER
ONE

MAPLE LEAVES & BEAVERS

Where do you start when a country's bigger than the entire EU and 33 times as big as Italy?

Epic, wild and showstopping she may be…. but a warmer welcome you won't find anywhere. No need to be a stranger. Get to know just how maple-syrup sweet Canada is, right here.

POPULATION

Canada is GI-NORMOUS!

But only

37 million people

live there.

It has the fourth lowest population density on earth with 3.7 people per square km.

The United States has 35 people per square km.

WHO LIVES HERE?

Canada is one of the most multicultural countries in the world.

Canada's First Nations make up 4.9 per cent of the population.

Those who consider themselves Canadian make up 32 per cent.

Other demographics include:

English 18.3 per cent.
Scottish 13.9 per cent.
French 13.6 per cent.
Irish 13.4 per cent.
German 9.6 per cent.
Chinese 5.1 per cent.

The word Canada is derived from the Indigenous word *Kanata*, which means "settlement" or "village" in the language of the St. Lawrence Iroquoians.

There are three main branches of Indigenous Peoples in Canada:

First Nations, Métis, and Inuit.

FIRST NATIONS

First Nations peoples originally settled in what is now known as Canada, mainly south of the Arctic Circle, many thousands of years ago, establishing trade routes and developing cultures and customs.

The ancestors of First Nations lived and thrived on traditional territories, which still hold a great deal of cultural and spiritual significance today.

INUIT

Inuit (Inuktitut for "the people") are an Indigenous people who are native to, and mostly inhabit, the Arctic and northern regions of present-day Canada.

Honed over thousands of years, Inuit are known for their incredible hunting and expert carving skills that have blossomed into a rich culture of diverse artistry, resourcefulness, and community.

MÉTIS

The Métis peoples are distinctly known for their mixed Indigenous and European ancestry, creating a unique and rich Métis culture of fiddle playing, dancing, and decorative art.

Métis roots are deeply connected to what are now the three Prairie provinces and parts of Ontario, British Columbia, and the Northwest Territories.

Canada spreads across six different
time zones, so regions are still enormous.
But Canadian's are helpful, so each
region is further divided into provinces
and territories:

ATLANTIC
Nova Scotia
New Brunswick
Prince Edward Island
Newfoundland
and Labrador

PRAIRIE PROVINCES
Manitoba
Saskatchewan
Alberta

CENTRAL CANADA
Quebec
Ontario

WEST COAST
British Columbia

NORTH
Yukon Territory
Northwest Territory
Nunavut

Each province or territory has its own capital city.

Nova Scotia	**Halifax**
New Brunswick	**Fredericton**
Prince Edward Island	**Charlottetown**
Newfoundland and Labrador	**St. John's**
Quebec	**Québec City**
Ontario	**Toronto**
Manitoba	**Winnipeg**
Saskatchewan	**Regina**
Alberta	**Edmonton**
British Columbia	**Victoria**
Yukon Territory	**Whitehorse**
Northwest Territory	**Yellowknife**
Nunavut	**Iqaluit**

66

I love Canada.
It's a wonderful
political act of faith
that exists atop
a breathtakingly
beautiful land.

99

Yann Martel

Canada has the longest coastline
of any country in the world,

151,019 miles!

It has three ocean borders:

The Pacific Ocean in the west

The Atlantic Ocean in the east.

The Arctic Ocean in the north.

Canada has 20 per cent of the world's fresh water and 0.5 per cent of the world's population.

However only seven per cent of the water is renewable.

The rest is "fossil water" stored in glaciers, underground aquifers and lakes.

Canada has around
2 million lakes,
more than
any other country.

Canada's National emblem is the maple leaf

Half of Canada is covered with forests, which amounts to 10 per cent of the world's forests. Most of it is publicly owned and can be explored.

1. The Carolinian Forest

2. St. Lawrence Forest

3. Boreal Forest

4. Mountain Forest

5. West Coast Forest

6. Columbia Forest

7. Montane Forest

8. Subalpine Forest

Canada's land border with the United States is the longest international border in the world at **5,525 miles.**

> ❝
> Canada is not a
> county for the
> cold of heart or
> the cold of feet.
> ❞

Pierre Trudeau

CLIMATE

Canada is huge and its climate varies, but it is largely characterized by freezing winters.

This is caused by:

1. Canada's latitude.

2. The Rocky Mountains that block the flow of mild Pacific air.

3. There are no topographic barriers blocking cold air masses from the North Pole.

SEASONS

Seasonal changes vary greatly.
Rules of thumb are…

Winter: December to February – but could be November to April – long, cold, lots of snow.

Spring: March to May – unpredictable, snow to sunshine in a day.

Summer: June to August – hot, humid weather, long days in the north.

Fall: September to November – leaves turn orange, red, and yellow, weather tends to be mild.

LAND OF
THE SILVER BIRCH

"Land of the Silver Birch,
Home of the Beaver,

Where Still the Mighty Moose
Wanders at Will,

Blue Lake and Rocky Shore,

I Will Return Once More."

**Traditional Canadian folk song
from the 1920s**

Like most traditional
songs, the lyrics
of "Land of the Silver
Birch" may differ
slightly in the various
regions of Canada.

"

If you don't like the weather, wait five minutes.

"

Canadian proverb

> **66**
> Not until I came
> to Canada did I
> realize that snow was
> a four-letter word.
> **99**

Canadian-Argentine writer Alberto Manguel,

CONFUSION

Canada is part of the British Commonwealth but the United States is their neighbour. They use the metric system and the imperial system.

Canadians follow speed limits and measure length in metres, but measure height in feet.

They check the temperature outside in Celsius, but cook in Fahrenheit.

They buy food by the kilogram, but weigh themselves in pounds.

"

Every Canadian has a complicated relationship with the United States, whereas Americans think of Canada as the place where the weather comes from.

"

Margaret Atwood, Ottawa

Canada's lowest
ever recorded
temperature was

-63°C

GOVERNMENT

1. Canada is a parliamentary democracy. Citizens vote in elections. The Prime minister is head of government.

2. Canada is a constitutional monarchy. The King of the UK is head of state.

3. Canada is one of the oldest continuing monarchies in the world (*French and British*).

66

The great tragedy of Canada
was the country could have had
British government, French
culture, and American efficiency,
but instead ended up with
French government, American
culture, and British efficiency.

99

Nick Auf de Maur
Journalist and politician

Canada is the number
one consumer of donuts
in the world.

30 million people eat
1 billion donuts a year.

LANGUAGE

French and English are the two official languages of the modern Canadian state.

Signage, commercial packaging, labels, government forms, and ATMs are all bilingual.

86 per cent of Canadians speak English while 30 per cent speak French.

There are also 11 different Indigenous language groups, which can be broken down further into 65 languages.

On top of this, there are over 128 additional languages spoken in Canada by people of other cultures.

What do you call a French Canadian who can speak English?

Bilingual

What do you call an English Canadian who can speak French?

A miracle

BEAVERS

This buck-toothed, semi-aquatic rodent is Canada's official national animal.

Beavers are known for using their teeth to chew through trees; a single beaver can fell 216 trees up to 40 cm in diameter in a single year!

Consumption
of macaroni and
cheese in Canada
is the highest
of any nation in
the world.

"

Canadians have been so busy
explaining to the Americans
that we aren't British, and to the
British that we aren't Americans,
that we haven't had time to
become Canadians.

"

Helen Gordon McPherson

CANADA DAY

Marking the country's day of confederation and the enactment of a self-governing nation, Canada Day is celebrated on July 1 with vibrant parades, delicious barbecues, and magical firework displays. The biggest celebration typically takes place in Parliament Hill, Ottowa.

Canada Day also provides an opportunity to reflect on and celebrate the diverse values of the country, including the significant contributions and culturally historic past of the Indigenous communities and the multicultural society who have shaped the nation.

The entire month of June is designated National Indigenous History Month to raise awareness of Indigenous Canadian cultures and customs, and to highlight current issues they may be facing.

66

Canada is free
and freedom is its
nationality.

99

Wilfred Laurier PM

NATIONAL INDIGENOUS PEOPLES DAY

Celebrated each year on
June 21 to honour those who
first carved communities on
this unique land.

The Indigenous name for
Canada is Turtle Island, and
on this Summer Solstice day,
Indigenous peoples across the
country hold celebrations,
ceremonies, performances,
and displays to honour their
homeland.

"

The seemingly interminable line of trees before you; the boundless wilderness around you; the mysterious depths amid the multitudinous foliage, where foot of man hath never penetrated… the solitude in which we proceeded mile after mile, no human being, no human dwelling within sight.

"

Anna Brownell Jameson 1837

THE NATIONAL ANTHEM
"O Canada"

O Canada!
Our home and native land!
True patriot love in all of us command.

With glowing hearts we see thee rise,
The True North strong and free!

From far and wide,
O Canada, we stand on guard for thee.

God keep our land glorious and free!
O Canada, we stand on guard for thee.

O Canada, we stand on guard for thee.

CHAPTER
TWO

MUST SEES

What people have seen, wish they'd seen, or go back to see. This is it. Twenty-one must-sees for the can-doers.

A (non-exhaustive) collection of unmissable places to visit, movies to watch, and activities that'll knock you right off those chunky hiking boots.

ROAD TRIP

The Trans Canada Highway
is Canada's longest road trip,
taking you coast to coast
through the cities of Montreal,
Ottawa, Calgary, and Vancouver
and into the world class
national parks of Banff, Yoho,
and Gros Morne.

THE ROCKIES

Banff, Yoho, Kootenay, and Jasper National Parks cross a mountain range that forms the British Columbia and Alberta border.

Whether you're after hiking, powder snow, glacial lakes, or white-water; you will find it here.

NIAGARA FALLS

Home of Horseshoe falls, one of the continent's most famous spectacles. A million bathtubs a second take a straight drop over a 54-metre cliff.

Iconic landmark and breathtaking views. Bring your raincoat.

OLD QUEBEC CITY

On the banks of the
St. Lawrence River is North
America's only walled city.

Over 400 years old, the old
town is a world heritage site.
Spired cathedrals, labyrinthian
lanes, street performers,
flaky pastries, and classical
architecture provide a
distinctive European feel.

10 MOVIES YOU DIDN'T KNOW WERE FILMED IN CANADA

Twilight (2008)	Vancouver and Lower Mainland
Juno (2007)	Vancouver
Brokeback Mountain (2005)	Rocky Mountains
Capote (2005)	Winnipeg and Manitoba
Mean Girls (2004)	Toronto
My Big Fat Greek Wedding (2002)	Toronto
Catch Me If You Can (2002)	Quebec
American Psycho (2000)	Toronto
Titanic (1997)	Halifax
Good Will Hunting (1997)	Toronto

DAWSON CITY

Subarctic scenery. Wild west feel. End of the line location.

Klondike-era buildings, icy rivers, and a saloon with poker and cancan dancers give this city a seductive, funky, and historic vibe.

CHURCHILL

Skilled hunters. Acute sense of smell. Razor sharp claws. 1,300 lbs and 10 ft tall. Lords of the arctic. Beyond the tree zone onto the edge of the tundra of Hudson Bay is Churchill, population 820.

The polar bear capital of the world: smack in the middle of the migration. Mid October to November is prime time to see polar bears.

66

Walk a mile in my moccasins to learn where they pinch.

99

Canadian Proverb

MONTREAL JAZZ FESTIVAL

Plug into this. Normally held in late June/early July, for 11 days 3,000 of the world's best jazz influenced muso's belt out jazz and blues across 650 concerts, most outdoors and free.

Good natured crowds. Multiple venues. Pure gold.

LEAF PEEPING

Autumn in Canada is a feast of foliage. Typically, from the end of September to the end of October, yellow birch, maples, pines, cedars, elms, oaks, spruce, and larch trees change colour.

Though Canada's half-covered in forests, Fundy Coast, Muskoka Lakes, and Cape Brereton are favourite spots.

BAFFIN ISLAND

Auyuittuq National Park.
"The land that never melts."
Truly remarkable.

Climb up high mountain
passes, base jump, cross rivers,
dodge polar bears, ice-fish,
or just be awestruck at brutal
glaciers, fjords, vertical cliffs,
and the Inuit that live and
survive here.

BAY OF FUNDY

Whether you understand the centrifugal force of the moon or not, a billion tonnes of water entering the Bay of Fundy is not something to be sneezed at.

It's the world's highest tide and one of the natural wonders of the world.

WHALE WATCHING

The East and West coast both provide food-rich waters and numberless sheltered bays that form the main migration routes for orcas, humpbacks, finback, blue, minke, and beluga whales.

Up close and personal, it's a mind-blowing experience as they dive, fluke, and blow. You can also see seal, porpoise, and dolphins.

TORONTO ART GALLERY

Frank Gehry's architectural fingerprints are all over this revamp with a four-storey titanium and glass wing plus a striking wood and glass north façade.

A permanent collection of over 120,000 works chart Canada's course from the first century to today. Seminal works, iconic renderings of wilderness, sculptures, and contemporary art.

FOGO ISLAND

Clean air, salty ocean, friendly people. The flat-earthers society proclaimed Fogo one of the four corners of the world. Grab a fish cake with salted cod, potatoes, and mustard.

Tilt your head back to see skies full of colourful Atlantic puffins and seabirds. Listen to an aquamarine iceberg calving in the wind-whipped North Atlantic.

WESTERN BROOK POND

Water falling 2,000 feet over billion-year-old cliffs into dark blue water framed by mighty mountains, hanging valleys, and huge rockslides.

Extraordinary landscape.
Jaw-dropping hiking trails
and boat rides.
Gros Morne National Park.

HAIDA GWAII "THE CANADIAN GALAPAGOS"

Haida Gwaii is an adventurer's paradise.

A stunning archipelago of islands off the British Columbian coast, the Haida Gwaii - formerly known as the Queen Charlotte Islands – has been home to the Haida Nation for over 10,000 years.

A moody, mystical, and magical experience awaits the Haida Gwaii visitor.

Haida Gwaii means "islands of the people" and access is by boat or seaplane only.

Around 5,000 people live all year round on the islands, of which roughly half are indigenous to Haida.

The islands are affectionately known as the "Canadian Galapagos" due to their staggering diversity.

CALGARY STAMPEDE, "GREATEST OUTDOOR SHOW ON EARTH"

Grab your Stetson and practice your yahoo – cowboys and girls are alive and well in Canada and are no better represented than at the annual Calgary Stampede, held every July.

A horse-soaked summer festival of traditional rodeo attractions, the Stampede attracts a remarkable million visitors, sometimes more, per year.

First Nations troupes, real-life cowboys, the Royal Mounted Police, bands, politicians, and businessmen all come together for this audio-visual spectacle like no other.

"

I believe the world needs more Canada.

"

Bono

KHUTZEYMATEEN GRIZZLY BEAR SANCTUARY

In a remote valley lies the only grizzly bear sanctuary in Canada. It protects British Columbia's largest-known coastal grizzly bear population.

Over 50 grizzlies live on this 45,000-hectare refuge. Watch them eat, play, and forage on the water's edge. Access by boat or float plane.

CANADIAN SLANG FOR GETTING AROUND

Eh   end of statement add-on to indicate question, affirmation or emphasis

Loonie   Canadian dollar coin

Toonie   two dollar coin

Washroom   toilet

Clicks   kilometres

Hang a Larry   turn left

Hang a Roger   turn right

Parkade   parking garage

Fill Yer Boots   help yourself

Jesus Murphy   satisfying curse without the guilt

GEORGIAN BAY ISLANDS

The world's largest freshwater archipelago. Between Honey Harbour and Twelve Mile Bay, there are 60 islands and many walking trails that take you from beaches to stands of white pines, Beech and Maple, bare granite cliffs, hemlock groves, wetland, forests, and marsh. Cycle along tracks, walk down trails or canoe emerald waters to glimpse the granite shores.

THE LAURENTIANS

One of the world's oldest mountain ranges. 500 million years of eroded and smoothed out rolling mountainsides, tranquil crystal-blue lakes by the hundred, meandering rivers, and endless coniferous forests with the towns and villages spotted throughout. Hike, bike, camp, canoe, eat, or ski.

DINOSAUR PROVINCIAL PARK

18,000 years ago, a glacial flood cut a ravine through the prairies creating this UNESCO World Heritage Site with one of the highest concentrations of dinosaur fossils in the world.

Multi-hued canyons and amazing rock formations. See a real dino leg just sitting there! Once in a lifetime stuff.

CHAPTER
THREE

ROAD TRIPS & ROLLING STOCK

A pair of hiking boots will only get you so far in a country that's 50 per cent permafrost, with 60 per cent of the world's polar bears, four mountain ranges, and the world's largest freshwater lakes.

Why not take a load off your feet and watch the surreal landscapes fly right by you.

ROAD TRIPS

What better way to explore than with a front row seat?

With over
9.8 million
square kilometres to choose from, here's a four-wheel adventure bucket list from black top to off the beaten track. Grab supplies and start your engines.

SEA TO SKY HIGHWAY BRITISH COLUMBIA

121 km of spectacle from Vancouver to Whistler. Takes anything from a two hour drive to five day hike, depending on how much you want to gape, eat, and walk.

Dramatic mountain scenery, the Pacific Ocean, Howe Sound, forests, fjords, and waterfalls. World class.

THE CABOT TRAIL

A 300 km coastal loop joining eight previously isolated fishing villages. One of the best road trips in the world, according to *Lonely Planet*.

It winds along the Margaree River, a Canadian Heritage River known for its long history of salmon fishing, and through the spectacular rugged highlands of the Cape Breton Highlands National Park. Think days of oysters, lobster, crab, mussels, salmon, pubs, and music.

Plus, you can go whale-watching, hiking, skiing, canoeing, golfing, horseback riding, fly-fishing, birding, or even kayaking. Festivals occur all along the trail. Work up an appetite dancing to Celtic music, dodging a moose, or spotting a bald eagle. There will always be a plate of lobster waiting!

KLONDIKE HIGHWAY YUKON

Skagway to Dawson City; 708 km in two days. Following in the footsteps of stampeding prospectors in the klondike gold rush, Highway 2 takes in alpine scenery, spectacular viewpoints, lakes, boreal forests, and high open valleys, before ending in the wild west town of Dawson City.

66

Isn't it nice to think that tomorrow is a new day with no mistakes in it yet?

99

Lucy Maud Montgomery
Canadian author of *Anne of Green Gables*, 1908

ICEFIELDS PATHWAY ALBERTA

230 km of double lane highway linking Banff and Jasper National Parks. 5–6 hours.

Pass 100 ancient glaciers, thundering waterfalls, cerulean lakes, and sweeping valleys of larch and pine.

Plenty of hikes and scenic viewpoints. Breathtakingly pristine rocky-mountain wilderness.

> **❝**
>
> Canada is the essence of not being. Not English. Not American. It is the mathematics of not being.
>
> **❞**

Mike Myers

VIKING TRAIL
NEWFOUNDLAND

Deer Lake to St. Anthony.
416 km. Drive there in five
hours or five weeks – your call.
From Deer Lake through Gros
Morne National Park to a small
fishing village perfect for whale
watching. Iceberg festivals,
rare plants, ancient Viking
settlements, and a supernatural
national park, Newfoundlands
route 430 is epic.

GASPÉSIE TOUR
QUEBEC

822 km. Three days to two weeks. If you fancy French Canadian culture, seaside villages, bonfires on the beach, Nordic spring rolls, lobster club sandwiches, and turquoise water this could be for you.

Stroll boardwalks, climb viewing points, hike trails, browse art galleries, whale watch, eat, and repeat.

COQUILLES AUX FRUITS DE MER

A classic of French cuisine found traditionally in this area.

Local Nordic shrimp and scallops cooked in a creamy sauce topped with fluffy mashed potatoes, heaps of Gruyere cheese, and broiled until golden and bubbly. Top up the cholesterol and hike it off the next day in Quebec.

66

In the European tradition, rivers are seen as divisions between peoples. But in the Aboriginal tradition, rivers are seen as the glue, the highway, the linkage between people, not the separation. And that's the history of Canada: our rivers and lakes were our highways.

99

John Ralston Saul
in an interview with Kate Fillion, *Maclean*,
September 25, 2008

LAKE SUPERIOR COASTLINE, ONTARIO

Sault Ste Marie to Thunder Bay. 700 km in two days. The Trans-Canada highway takes you alongside the world's largest freshwater lake.

Through Pancake, Lake Superior, and Rocky Neys provincial parks. En-route, you'll find Indigenous rock pictographs, fur trading posts, mind-blowing stargazing, cliffs, hiking trails, moose, lynx, black bears, and Canadian wolves.

"

Canadians are simply disarmed Americans with health care.

"

Anonymous

THE DEMPSTER HIGHWAY, YUKON

Dawson city to Inuvik. 740 km. The Dempster Highway is hard-packed gravel through the Ogilvie and Richardson mountains.

The road crosses the continental divide three times and traverses the arctic circle, loosely following old dog team routes to Inuvik. Scenic. Remote. Wild. Grizzly bears, black bears, foxes, wolves, caribou, and rabbits.

INGRAHAM TRAIL

Yellowknife to Tibbitt Lake. 70 km. A storied route winding through nine parks and a dozen lakes with colourful wildlife and world-class fishing.

Prime viewing location for the Northern Lights during aurora season. Gateway to hidden-gem canoe trips. Granite hills and woodlands, boreal forests, blue lakes, wild berries, and rocky shores are never far away.

> **"**
>
> To survive the Canadian winter, one needs a body of brass, eyes of glass, and blood made of brandy.
>
> **"**

Louis Armand de Lom d'Arce Lahontan, 1702

"

Agreeable people are warm and friendly. They're nice; they're polite. You find a lot of them in Canada.

"

Adam Grant

ICE ROAD, NORTHWEST TERRITORIES

Inuvik to Aklavik. 117 km.
Every winter, 2,000 km of ice roads
are ploughed across frozen waterways
connecting 12 isolated towns in
Canada's vast Northwest Territories.

From late December to early April,
you can cross the Mackenzie delta
while gawping at the Richardson
Mountains. Stunning views north of
the arctic circle. Cold. Dark. Average
speeds of 50 km/h. Head over in April
to experience the big jamboree known
as the Mad Trapper Rendezvous.

COWBOY TRAIL

Cardston Alberta to Mayerthorpe. 700km in 7–8 days. Between the Rocky Mountains and the Canadian prairie is the high ranching country of Alberta. It's known for its mixed forests, grasslands, and down-home ranch-style cooking after a day on the trail. Fishing or trail riding. Casino or rock climbing. Rodeo or festival. The old west is still alive. There are medicine walks and Tee Pee pow wows. Saddle up!

The Trans-Canada
highway is

4,860

miles long.

GRASSLANDS NATIONAL PARK

One or two days. 268 km. Saskatchewan's see the east block's wild and fragile prairie landscape from Badlands Pathway.

Expect plains bison, black-footed ferrets, and settler homesteads in the West Block Ecotour Scenic drive.

IRISH LOOP, NEWFOUNDLAND AND LABRADOR

A 309 km coastal loop starting from the capital St. John's. Past the oldest European settlements in North America and treacherous seas with their lighthouse guardians.

Walk coastal trails with towering cliffs, fjords, sea stacks, rock arches, and geysers. Watch 10,000-year-old icebergs drift past millions of seabirds and thousands of humpback and minke whales feeding at the Witless Bay Ecological Reserve.

BEST TRAIN TRIPS

Canada boasts some of the best railway trips on the planet. Frontier engineering. Marvels of nature. Seasonal changes. Bespoke trains.

Short, overnight or odyssey. Prairies, mountains, or coast. A great way to see a big country.

MONTREAL TO HALIFAX ON THE OCEAN

1,346 km in 20 hours. Canada's classic overnight rail trip. Think meals in mid-century rail dining cars, glass-domed observation cars, and private sleeper cabins. Gulf of St. Lawrence. The Miramichi River. Sugarloaf Mountain. Epic eye-candy. A leaf peeper's heaven in the fall.

WINNIPEG TO CHURCHILL

1,697 km in 36 hours. From the capital of Manitoba province all the way to the Western shores of Hudson Bay. Can be slow because of frost on the tracks, but luckily you can admire the Northern landscapes.

Get blown away by the tundra, aurora borealis, herds of caribou, beluga whales, and polar bears.

VANCOUVER TO TORONTO ON "THE CANADIAN"

4,466 km in 96 hours. Restored stainless steel carriages in an Art Deco style, this is nostalgic and luxury long-distance rail travel.

From the observation car or lounge, travel over the Rockies across the prairies and scenic lake lands. Forests. River valleys. Waterfalls. Grazing animals. Mountain peaks. Saxophone players helping you down pan roasted halibut or a prime rib of beef. Too easy.

JASPER TO PRINCE RUPERT ON THE RUPERT ROCKET

1,160 km in two days. Travel northwest past Mount Robson and the Caribou mountains. From vintage steel-sided carriages see white-tailed deer, black bears, moose, and bald eagles. Not to mention the glassy lakes, fir trees, and gritty backcountry. Some of the most spectacular mountain scenery in Canada. Romance of a true rail adventure.

THE ROCKY MOUNTAINEER

One or two nights. Private rail offering three different routes through the Rockies. Overnight in hotels so you don't miss a second of mind-blowing scenery during the day. Huge windows, top notch tucker, booze, and open-air viewing platforms. Lake shores, mountains, bridges, lava cliffs, canyons, ospreys, bald eagles, and engineering feats.

CHAPTER
FOUR

PLACES, PARKS & POUTINE

Wrap your head around this nation's
major cities. Scratch your head
at her natural wonders. Lick your lips
at her regional cuisine.

Flipper pie anyone?

EIGHT BIGGEST CITIES

Toronto

Half of the population of Canada's largest city were born somewhere else. Over 140 languages are spoken in a 21 by 43 km block, making it the world's most multicultural city.

Ontarians are known as mild-mannered, hockey mad, and outdoor loving.

Calgary

Canada's wild west, "Cowtown", has been ranked as the world's fifth most liveable city seven times in a row. Calgary is the youngest and warmest city in Canada, with 333 sunny days per year.

Cool eateries, nightlife, and a can-do cowboy attitude. Host of the Calgary Stampede, one of Canada's biggest parties.

Ottawa

The nation's capital is on the Ottawa River and Rideau Canal. A place of world class museums, gothic parliament buildings, architecturally-inspiring homes, parks, gardens, and wide-open spaces.

Take a walk along the river, check out the ice sculptures at Winterlude festival, skate to town along the canal, and check out the tulips and fall leaves.

Edmonton

The country's largest northernmost city is a vibrant urban centre in the heart of the wilderness.

Known as "the Gateway to the North", Edmonton boasts the most sunshine in Canada – 18 hours in the summer – and the biggest mall in North America.

Canada's festival city; it hosts over 50 festivals annually. Glamping under the aurora, farmers markets, Jasper National Park. Nice.

Mississauga

On the shores of Lake Ontario, the eclectic neighborhoods, beautiful waterfront, and thriving business community attract a multicultural population.

World class shopping, historic neighborhoods, over 500 parks, gardens and trails, and 30 km of water frontage.

Winnipeg

Bustling and picturesque city in the heart of the country. The Royal Canadian Mint, Winnipeg Zoo, galleries, and museums.

With 640 acres of prairie in the city itself, watch bison roam and birds migrate.

Rug up during the winter. Take a horse-drawn sleigh ride. See the northern lights. Cheer for the Jets. Catch Folkorama, the largest multicultural festival in the world.

Montreal

The Paris of Canada. The nation's second largest city with a rich culture, history, and reputation for lively night life.

Big on outdoor activities and a serious passion for food. Do not debate where the world's best bagels, maple syrup, poutine, or smoked meats come from.

The city of Montreal regularly appears on global lists of most liveable and happiest places.

Vancouver

Beaches, islands, coastline, and mountains… it's sea to sky beauty by a laid-back city and suburbs.

Ski in the morning and surf in the afternoon. Hike, bike, windsurf, or kayak. Whale watch. Drink and dine to dramatic vistas.

The most popular filming location after New York and LA. Mild weather. Wow.

NATIONAL PARKS IN CANADA

In the late 1800s, under pressure from mining, logging, railroads, cities, and factories, a land preservation movement emerged that was ahead of its time. The brief was to protect land that was important, remarkable or threatened. This has burgeoned into the world class national parks system managed by the federal government.

TOP 10 MOST POPULAR NATIONAL PARKS

1. Banff National Park, AB
2. Yoho National Park, B.C.
3. Pacific Rim National Park Reserve, B.C.
4. Jasper National Park, AB
5. Gros Morne National Park, N.L.
6. Fundy National Park, N.B.
7. Bruce Peninsula National Park, ON
8. Ivvavik National Park, YT
9. Nahanni National Park Reserve, N.T.
10. Waterton Lakes National Park, AB

NATIONAL PARKS

38 national parks. More than 130,000 square miles of wilderness. Millions of annual visitors. Moose. Turtle. Beaver. Whale. Bison. Wolf. Bear – polar, grizzly, and black.

Canada's national parks are of immense international importance and house some of the planet's most incredible wildlife. An experience that will stay with you forever.

IN CANADA'S NATIONAL PARKS YOU COULD FIND YOURSELF...

Hiking
Cycling
Camping
Skiing
Snowshoeing
Mountain-climbing

Kayaking
Canoeing
Motorboating
Scuba diving
Surfing
Snowmobiling
Dog sledding

Some national parks are entirely untouched wilderness with no man-made facilities. They are accessible only by boat or plane:

Aulavik

Akami-Uapishkᵘ-KakKasuak-Mealy Mountains

Ivvavik

Nááts'ihch'oh

Nahanni

Other national parks are
developed resort towns with
modern shops, restaurants,
and hotels:

Yoho

Waterton Lakes

Terra Nova

Banff

Riding Mountain

Jasper

EVERY CANADIAN NATIONAL PARK HAS SOMETHING UNIQUE TO OFFER

Clear waters, highlands, marsh, grasslands, rocky cliffs, beaches, exotic flora and fauna, arctic mountains, ice fields, rivers, canyons, hot springs fjords, waterfalls, wildflowers, meadows, rocky bluffs, dry tundras, glaciers, iceberg-filled waters, wetlands, orchards, canyons, vast forests, treeless barren tundra, and mountain ranges.

ANOTHER
10 NATIONAL PARKS

1. Auyuittuq National Park, NU

2. Prince Edward Island National Park, P.E.

3. Cape Breton Highlands
National Park, N.S.

4. Wapusk National Park, MB

5. Bruce Peninsula National Park, ON

6. Grasslands National Park, SK

7. Prince Edward Island, P.E.

8. Fathom Five National Marine Park, ON

9. Mount Revelstoke and Glacier, B.C.

10. Saguenay-St. Lawrence Marine Park, QC

FOOD BY REGION

No matter what type of adventure you're having, there's nothing better than pulling up a stool and sharing a plate of the region's cuisine with a friendly Kanuck. It's even better when you know what the menu is saying.

Here are some tips to help your tastebuds navigate the country.

FOODY SLANG

A Two Four	case of 24 beers
Suitcase	12 beers
Molson Muscle	beer gut
Mickey	hipflask of spirits
Texas Mickey	3 litre bottle of liquor
Pop	soda
Timmies	favourite national coffee store
Timbit	round donut hole
Double Double	coffee with two creams and two sugars
Back Bacon	pork product
Dart	cigarette
Kraft Dinner or KD	packaged macaroni and cheese, considered de facto national dish

QUEBEC
Poutine "poo-teen"

Thick-cut golden fries served with melted cheese curds, and salty gravy.

Eaten with fork.

High in carbs, fat, and protein.

Perfect.

POUTINE RECIPE

1. Add hot, cooked fries to a large bowl.

2. Season lightly with salt.

3. Pour in a ladle of hot gravy and toss. Add more gravy as needed to coat the fries.

4. Add cheese curds and toss.

5. Serve with freshly ground pepper.

BRITISH COLUMBIA
Nanaimo Bars

Iconic Canadian dessert.

Three layered no-bake bar.

Wafer crumb and coconut base, custard butter icing, and a chocolate ganache top.

B.C. SPECIALS

West Coast Fish Chowder

Smoked, candied salmon, and rockfish in a
medley of potatoes fennel, celery, onions,
bacon, and cream.

Hot Smoked Salmon Sandwich

Wild, smoked salmon, maple mustard,
coleslaw, and spicy Sriracha mayo layered on
a ciabatta bun.

Seared Albacore Tuna Loin

Buttery Pacific Tuna seared, sliced crosswise
and smothered in gingery-garlic ponzu sauce.

YUKON FAVOURITES

The Yukon's clean water, soil and natural forests mean unforgettable flavours.

Smoked salmon with wild birch sauce.

Wild Yukon raspberries.

Elk sausage rolls.

Bannock flatbreads.

Snow ice cream.

NORTHWEST TERRITORIES
Famous for fish

Warm up with a bowl of Moose stew or the freshest fish you've ever eaten. Northern pike, pickerel, grayling, Arctic char, and lake trout are specialties.

Or go full traditional with musk ox or moose steaks cooked on a wood stove.

PRINCE EDWARD ISLAND

Full lobster supper is a staple.

Lobster roll: lobster chunks, lettuce, mayo, and a soft roll.

Oysters from Malpeque Bay, Raspberry Point, and Colville Bay are world famous.

COWS ice cream is rumoured to be the best in Canada.

Raspberry cream cheese pies, jams, jellies, crisp, and cobblers.

Fries With The Works (FWTW) includes fries topped with gravy, canned peas, and island ground beef.

ALBERTA

Bison: tenderloin, short ribs, and burgers.

Creamy white honey.

Red fife wheat in sourdough baguettes and croissants.

Saskatoon berries: wild, deep blue berries with an earthy flavour.

ONTARIO

Raymond Massey

Rye whiskey and ginger syrup shaken with ice and topped with champagne and a lemon garnish.

Peameal Bacon Sandwich

Thick slices of fatty bacon rolled in ground yellow peas on a kaiser bun.

Sushi pizza

A fried rice patty topped with salmon, tuna, crab, avocado slices, spicy mayonnaise, and soy-wasabi sauce.

MANITOBA

Lean bison meat.

Schmoo torte: layers of sponge, whipped cream, nuts, and plenty of melted caramel sauce.

Goldeye fish: marinated in brine, slightly dried, and then smoked over cherry wood.

Honey dill mayonnaise.

Bothwell cheese.

Slurpees.

Fatboy burgers.

NEWFOUNDLAND AND LABRADOR

10,000-year-old pre-industrial revolution water makes the best Iceberg vodka and Iceberg beer, perfect to wash down a plate of flipper pie or cod tongues.

Scrunchion's are plates of fried pork backfat. Rumoured to cure hangovers.

Don't forget your greens — oyster leaf and caribou moss.

NOVA SCOTIA

Nova salmon: brined and cold-smoked. Unique mild flavour and firm flesh.

Moosehunters cookies.

Halifax Donair: crisp, seasoned beef with freshly chopped onion and tomato sauce on pita bread.

Moon Mist: ice cream.

Rappie Pie: unique potatoe and chicken pie with no crust.

Hodge Podge: veg stew made in spring with the freshest veg.

Meat paste egg rolls.

SASKATCHEWAN

Saskatoon: Berry pie, wine, and jam.

Bison, geese, and duck are all on the menu.

With over 100,000 lakes, all the fish are fresh: walleye, lake trout, northern pike, Arctic grayling.

Shishliki.

Spudnuts.

Perogies, borscht, and cabbage rolls.

Deer sausage.

Chokecherries in jellies, jams, juices, syrups, and wines.

Pemmican-lean meat, dried pounded, and mixed with fat and berries.

" Canada is the best country in the world. "

Justin Bieber, Canadian Singer

NUNAVUT

Think hearty, belly-warming foods
from subsistence living.

Caribou stew.

Roasted musk ox.

Mussels, clams, turbot, Greenland
shrimp.

Stewed dried or baked Arctic char.

Raw whale blubber.

Blue, black, cran, and Baffin berries.

NEW BRUNSWICK

Poutine râpée: boiled potato dumpling with a filling of seasoned pork.

Coquille Saint Jacques: poached scallops in a wine sauce topped with breadcrumbs and cheese.

Fried clams.

Pets de sœur: cinnamon pinwheel pastry.

Cipâte: cubed potatoes, meat, and onions slow cooked between multiple layers of dough.

Ployes: buttered buckwheat pancake covered in either pork spread, maple syrup, brown sugar, or molasses.

CHAPTER
FIVE

PASTIMES & TOUCHSTONES

A taste of the nation's sweet-tooth, vices and wildly beautiful festivities.

Sit back and whip yourself up a hot maple toddy while you discover fascinating facts and original traditions of this sticky treat, along with possible life-saving survival tips (yes, you can fight off a cougar), and Canadian colloquialisms that'll make sure you fit right in with these loveable misfits.

POPULAR CANADIAN FESTIVALS #1

Winterlude

If you love snow, Canada's the place for you. Over three weekends in February, Ottawa hosts Winterlude — a head-spinning mix of indoor and outdoor entertainment, including live music and the world's largest skating rink at more than five miles long.

CELEBS

Canadians love to name drop one of their own into the conversation.

Margaret Atwood	Celine Dion
K.D. Lang	Ryan Gosling
Saul Bellow	Sandra Oh
Leonard Cohen	Jim Carrey
Lucy Maud Montgomery	Shania Twain
Justin Bieber	Keanu Reeves
Drake	Michael J Fox

MAPLE SYRUP "LIQUID GOLD"

Maple Syrup is synonymous with Canada and has long been recognized as a source of energy and nutrition.

There are no authenticated accounts of when maple syrup consumption and production began, but Indigenous oral traditions, together with archaeological evidence, certainly prove that maple syrup and maple sugar were being produced long before the European settlers arrived.

STICKY FACTS #1

The average Canadian
consumes about
2.4 litres of maple syrup
per year.

Maple trees are tapped for their syrup between late February and early April when the alternating night frosts and daytime thaws promote the flow of sap throughout the tree.

Under Canadian maple product regulations, quantities are always measured in litres. An average maple tree can produce up to 50 litres of sap a year.

Maple trees can live up to 200 years, but most are cut down after 75 because their yield declines.

STICKY FACTS #2

It takes 40 litres
of maple sap to make
just one litre of
Canadian maple syrup.

HOT MAPLE TODDY

Ingredients

1 cup whiskey
1 cup maple syrup
¾ cup lemon juice
1 slice butter
cinnamon stick (to garnish)

Directions

1. Combine all ingredients in a medium saucepan.

2. Simmer over low heat until flavours blend.

3. Serve hot in a cappuccino mug with a slice of butter and cinnamon stick.

TOP 12 MAPLES

1. Maple Syrup
2. Maple Butter
3. Maple Soft Sugar
4. Maple Hard Sugar
5. Maple Taffy
6. Maple Liqueur
7. Maple Beer
8. Maple BBQ Sauce
9. Maple Cookies
10. Hot Maple Toddy
11. Maple Bar (bacon optional)
12. Maple Syrup Soap

STICKY FACTS #3

Canadian Grade A maple syrup
has four classifications.

Golden – Delicate taste

Amber – Rich taste

Dark – Robust taste

Very Dark – Strong taste

POPULAR CANADIAN FESTIVALS #2

Quebec Winter Carnival

Quebecois go wild before Lent each year with food, drink, snow sculptures, night parades, canoe racing, and more skating. Held every year in January and February, this really is a winter wonderland.

TIRE D'ÉRABLE

A traditional Quebec delicacy is, literally, a pull of maple.

A thin 15 cm stream of hot syrup is poured on a bed of snow.

As the syrup cools and hardens, the lucky recipient uses a popsicle stick to roll the still pliable maple into a lollipop.

YUM.

FUNNY CANADIAN PLACES

1. St. Louis du Ha! Ha! – Quebec

2. Sexsmith- Alberta

3. Wawa – Ontario

4. Stoner – British Columbia

5. Climax – Saskatchewan

6. Head Smashed in Buffalo Jump – Alberta

7. Forget – Saskatchewan

8. Come by Chance – Newfoundland

9. Vulcan – Alberta

10. Nameless Cove – Newfoundland

11. Goobies – Newfoundland

12. Spread Eagle – Newfoundland

13. Dildo – Newfoundland

ANIMALS

Canada is world famous for its fauna for good reason. When you're out and about you might find yourself passing the day with a…

Moose
Polar Bear
Bison
Walrus
Beaver
Caribou
Atlantic Puffin
Massassaliga Rattlesnake

Prairie Rattlesnake
Cougar
Grizzly Bear
Black Bear
Wolf
Coyote
Canada Lynx
Beluga Whale

IN THE WILDS

Mosquitos and blackflies are probably the only things you'll need to swat away. But bears, cougars, and snakes live here, too.

Survival tactics

Cougars

Fight a cougar off, they usually avoid groups.

Bears

Hikers blow whistles to warn bears off.
If confronted, don't run, make loud noises, or sudden movements.

Snakes

Back away leaving room for snake to escape.

POPULAR CANADIAN FESTIVALS #3

Montreal Jazz Festival

The world's finest musicians have visited this festival over the years, with around 500 concerts held each year, entertaining millions. Former visitors include Mark Knopfler, Aretha Franklin, Ella Fitzgerald, Carole King, and Elton John.

STICKY FACTS #4

Canada produced a record-high 17.4 million gallons of maple syrup in 2022, with over 90 per cent produced in the Quebec province.

POPULAR CANADIAN FESTIVALS #4

Celebration of Light

Vancouver provides a fireworks spectacle like you've never seen. In fact, it's the world's biggest fireworks event, held over three nights each summer.

CANADIAN SLANG

Toque	wool hat
Gotch/Gitch/Gonch	underwear
Canuck	Canadian
Hoser	Canadian redneck
The Peg	Winnipeg
The 6ix	Toronto
Chesterfield	couch
Backpack	knapsack
Keener	brown noser
Beauty	a person or event that is exceptionally fine
British Californa	British Columbia

(known for its mild winters and laidback lifestyle)

12 BOOKS
SET IN CANADA

1. *The Shipping News*, Annie Proulx
2. *The Colony of Unrequited Dreams*,
   Wayne Johnston
3. *Anne of Green Gables*, Lucy Maud Montgomery
4. *The Blind Assassin*, Margaret Atwood
5. *The Stone Diaries*, Carol Shields
6. *The Break*, Katherena Vermette
7. *Bury Your Dead (Inspector Gamache Series)*,
   Louise Penny
8. *Lives of Girls and Women*, Alice Munro
9. *The Stone Angel*, Margaret Laurence
10. *Cape Breton Road*, D.R. MacDonald
11. *River Thieves*, Michael Crummey
12. *Annabel*, Kathleen Winter

POPULAR CANADIAN FESTIVALS #5

Toronto International Film Festival

Every September, stars from both behind and in front of the camera gather for one of the world's most prestigious film festivals. *American Beauty, Ray, The King's Speech, Slumdog Millionaire,* and *The Black Swan* have all premiered here.

WINE

Small scale production and clean air, soil, and water produce intriguing local flavours developing an international reputation.

Niagara Peninsula Ontario: More than 60 wineries grow three-quarters of Canada's grapes in a variety of soils and micro climates. Pinots' merlot and chardonnay. Block buster wineries with restaurants.

Prince Edward County Ontario: cool climate wines including chardonnay and pinot noir.

Quebec: Riesling and chardonnays. Regional specialties include ice wines, dessert wines, fruit wines, and cider.

Nova Scotia: cool climate whites and new world sparklings in one of the world's coldest grape growing areas.

La Route Des Vins (The Wine Route)

Snaking 120 km through the eastern townships, sip your way through Quebec's best at a dozen lush vineyards from Brome to Missisquoi.

B.C. BIG BUD TO ISLAND SKANK

Canada became the first G20 nation to legalize use of recreational marijuana in October 2018. It also passed a law allowing citizens with a criminal record for marijuana possession to be pardoned quickly and without cost. Around 50 per cent of Canadians have tried it. Around 15 per cent of Canadians use cannabis at least once a year.

The black market still flourishes, but eager entrepreneurs mean over-the-counter highs now come in a variety of forms: flowers, sublinguals, tinctures, vapes, carbonated beverages, cannabis-infused water, pre-rolls, extracts, concentrates, chocolates, gummies, capsules, soft chews, hard candies, fruit sticks, lattes, etc.

" Canadians are more polite when they are being rude than Americans are when they are being friendly. "

Edgar Friedenberg

CHAPTER

SIX

STICKS & PUCKS

Canadians may be a pretty laid-back lot, but only until someone mentions team rivalry. Temperatures rise. Cursing starts. Blood may be spilt.

Before you join in on the action, take a quick flip through to learn about a thousand-year-old Indigenous sport, tips on how to become a raging, die-hard fan at a Hockey game, or facts for a cultured dinner-table conversation about the best Ski resorts in this winter wonderland.

SPORTS

Canadians are mad about sports and play football (grid iron), baseball, basketball, soccer (football), and rodeo. Ice hockey, football, and baseball are the top spectator sports.

There are two official national sports: lacrosse in summer and ice hockey in winter.

❝

In Canada, its beer, hockey, and then everything else.

❞

Edge
Canadian wrestling professional and actor

ICE HOCKEY

Who would think a pair of skates, a frozen pond, a stick, and a puck could knit a country together?

Best time to rob a bank (in case you were wondering) is the ice hockey final: Canada shuts down. The scrape of skates. Cursing. Announcers giving you the play by plays.

Get to a game.

"
Hockey is our winter ballet and, in many ways, our only national drama.

"

Morley Callaghan, Writer

HOCKEY SLANG

Chirp	trash talk
Dangler	impressive puck manipulation
Flow	skaters' hair
Beauty	team player
Barn-burner	fast paced game
Biscuit	puck
Celly	celebration
Grocery stick	useless player
Pylon	lazy, stationary player
Tilt	fight
10 ply	emotionally soft
Five-hole	space between a goal keeper's legs

Gong Show	crazy
Out For a Rip	out for a good time
Kerfuffle	mix up
Rink Rat	enthusiastic ice skater
Deking	a decoy move
Goal Suck	goal potter who does not do their share of defense
Chirping	sledging
Puck Bunny	hockey team groupie
Git'r done	phrase of encouragement
Give'r	phrase of encouragement

PICK YOUR SIDE

There are seven Canadian teams in the 32 team North American NHL:

1. Calgary Flames

2. Edmonton Oilers

3. Montreal Canadiens

4. Ottawa Senators

5. Toronto Maple Leafs

6. Vancouver Canucks

7. Winnipeg Jets

"

Hockey players wear numbers because you can't always identify the body with dental records.

"

Anonymous

179

GOING TO A GAME

Wear heavy shoes, warm socks, gloves, and layers under a coat and a hat.

Arrive early and hungry.

Be prepared for knowledgeable fans, passion, and not a small amount of cursing.

> ## The only worse job is a javelin catcher at a track-and-field meet.

Hall of Famer Gump Worsley on goaltending

THE LOWDOWN

A match is three 20-minute periods with 20-minute intermissions: about 2 hours 15 minutes all in.

Six players from each team are on the ice at any time, but they swap constantly due to the pace of the game.

There are also face-offs, power plays, slapshots, icing, and much more... but this is only a little book.

> " All hockey players are bilingual. They know English and profanity. "

Gordie Howe

66

A puck is a hard rubber disc that hockey players strike when they can't hit one another.

99

Jimmy Cannon

> **66**
>
> Ninety percent of hockey is mental and the other half is physical..
>
> **99**

Wayne Gretzky

LACROSSE

Rival Indigenous communities would battle if they needed to — but settling minor disagreements was better done by organized games.

Lacrosse was one of these — a Haudenosaunee game played by the Five Nations when disputes needed to be settled.

Pre-dating recorded history, lacrosse was played on a huge "pitch", often several kilometres long, with up to 1,000 warriors and could last 2–3 days.

Lacrosse had an important role in the community, with a profound spiritual significance.

Today, this fast and furious sport is played worldwide, with four distinct versions played in Canada: men's field, women's field, box, and inter-crosse.

A team sport of 10 players a side, games are played over four quarters of 15 minutes each quarter.

"
If you can't play nice, play lacrosse.
"

Unknown

SKIING

With outstanding technical facilities, a variety of terrain, world class grooming, year-round snow, hundreds of lifts, and long runs… its little wonder why pros from around the world train in Canada.

Offering something for everyone from beginners to freestyle skiers and boarders, there's jumps, rails, an Olympic sized pipe, full-service resorts, and back country wilderness.

Whistler often tops the list of the world's best snowfields.

TOP 10 SKI RESORTS

1. Mont Tremblant

2. Mount Norquay, Banff

3. Kicking Horse

4. Big White

5. Whistler

6. Fernie Alpine

7. Sun peaks

8. Revelstoke

9. Panorama Mountain Resort

10. RED Mountain Resort

"

My dream is for people around the world to look up and to see Canada like a little jewel sitting at the top of the continent.

"

Tommy Douglas
Former Premier of Saskatchewan